D0818182

A Mule Named Sugar Cube

by Maria Fleming
illustrated by Margeaux Lucas

SCHOLASTIC INC.

New York • Toronto • London • Auckland • Sydney
Mexico City • New Delhi • Hong Kong • Buenos Aires

No part of this publication may be reproduced, or stored in a retrieval system, or transmitted in any form or by any means, electronic, mechanical, photocopying, recording, or otherwise, without written permission of the publisher. For information regarding permission, write to Scholastic Inc., Attention: Permissions Department, 557 Broadway, New York, NY 10012.

Designed by Maria Lilja
ISBN-13: 978-0-439-88461-7 • ISBN-10: 0-439-88461-6
Copyright © 2006 by Scholastic Inc.
All rights reserved. Printed in the U.S.A.

First printing, November 2006

12 11 10 9 8 7 6 5 4 3 2 1   6 7 8 9 10 11/0

Phonics Fact

This book is full of long-*u* words. Many times this sound is made by a silent *e*. The vowel *u* is followed by a consonant, which is then followed by a silent *e*, as in **cube** and **mule**. What other long-*u* words can you find in this story? Look at the pictures, too!

This is Sugar **Cube**. Sugar **Cube** is a very **cute mule**.

I'll have a **huge** bowl of sugar **cubes**.

Phonics Fact

The letter *u* does not always need the help of silent *e* to make the long-*u* sound. Sometimes a single *u* makes the sound all by itself. The word **unusual** has two long-*u* sounds in it! Can you find two words in the picture that use a single *u* to make the long-*u* sound?

(Answer: **Hugo's, menu**)

Sugar **Cube** is not like other **mules**.
Sugar **Cube** is **unusual**.

3

Sugar **Cube** can **use** a **computer**.

Sugar **Cube** loves **music**. She can play
the **bugle**.

Sugar **Cube** likes to go to the **museum**.

Sugar **Cube** can ride a **unicycle**.

Speech bubbles in illustration: "Hey, **you**!" "Mew!"

Phonics Fact

The letters *ew* sometimes make the long-*u* sound, as in **few**. The letters *you* also make the long-*u* sound, as in **youthful**. Can you find other long-*u* words on this page that use these spelling patterns?

(Answer: **mew, Matthew, you**)

One day, a **few youthful mules** call Sugar **Cube** over.

"**Excuse** me," says a **mule** named **Matthew**.

"But **you** should act like a **regular mule**."

Matthew hurt Sugar **Cube's** feelings. Sugar **Cube** wants to fit in. She wants to be part of the **mule community**.

Sugar **Cube** tries to do **regular mule** things. But it's no **use**. **Regular mule** things do not **amuse** her.

Then Sugar **Cube** gets a **useful** idea.

Sugar **Cube** teaches the other **mules** how to **use** a **computer**. She teaches them how to ride a **unicycle** and play the **bugle**.

Sugar **Cube** even takes the other **mules** to the **museum**. Now Sugar **Cube** is not such an **unusual mule**.

But she is still very **cute**!

Long-u Riddles

Listen to the riddles. Then match each riddle with the right long-*u* word from the box.

Word Box

cube	music	few	museum	menu
mule	huge	you	cute	computer

1 This farm animal looks kind of like a horse.

2 It is the opposite of *me*.

3 You use this to order food at a restaurant.

4 It means *very big*.

5 You can use this to write, play games, or send e-mail.

6 You can see art in this building.

7 This has a square shape.

8 It rhymes with *flute*.

9 It is the opposite of *many*.

10 You hear this on the radio.

Answers: 1. mule 2. you 3. menu 4. huge 5. computer 6. museum 7. cube 8. cute 9. few 10. music

15

Long-u Cheer

Hooray for long *u*, the best sound around!

Let's holler long-*u* words all over town!

There's **cube** and **cute** and **huge** and **mule**.

There's **music** and **bugle** and **menu** and **fuel**.

There's **fuse** and **fume** and **youth** and **few**.

There's **uniform**, **cucumber**, **perfume**, and **you**.

Long *u*, long *u*, give a great cheer,

For the most **useful** sound **you** ever will hear!

Make a list of other long-*u* words. Then use them in your cheer.